PRAISE

"Congratulations on a fine book that is destined to help many who take the time to apply your principles … *The Boyne Advantage* reflects so many human experiences: love, sorrow, frustration, the need for persistence, open-mindedness, the futility of self-pity …" –Joseph C. Dilger

"*The Boyne Advantage* is truly a motto for life. I always write it down, as a constant reminder of how grateful I am … and for all the lessons I can continue to learn each day."

–Sydney Bennet

"… very empowering." –Debbie Bartlett

"This story shares with readers how their lives can become meaningful … in a way they desire. Even at the age of ninety-two, I am still using the worksheets to improve my life.

–Anne Thurston

"I just finished reading *The Boyne Advantage*. It was fantastic!! It makes [one] put life in perspective." – Anneke Rader

"I have read many self-help books and I compliment you on the five simple steps … [working the principles] is like dropping a stone in the lake—the ripples go on and on. I believe everyone can benefit from [reading] it." –Gloria Westrick

"… so full of truths about life that sometimes get forgotten in the everyday chaos of life and the media." –Sue Hobbs

"This is the first book of this kind that I really enjoyed and actually wrote down what I am thankful for and proud of [accomplishing]. ... This is a wonderful gift and I will recommend this book to my family and friends." –Robbie Weiss

"I enjoyed your book very much and would recommend it to anyone to read ..." –Eleanor Sutliff

"I picked it up and couldn't put it down. I'm looking forward to sharing it with my boys. Thank you for making a difference."
–Leslie Neilson

"Very well done. I think you will help a lot of people refocus on values and personal goals!" –Dawn Noblett

the Boyne *Advantage*

the Boyne *Advantage*

5 Simple Steps for Achieving Success in Work and Life

Mark D. Kowalske

Second Edition 2015

**Author is available for speaking and training events.
For additional information and to contact the author,
email him at markkowalske@gmail.com**

Edition ISBNs:
Hard cover: 978-0-692-38087-1
Paperback: 978-0-615-77387-2

Library of Congress Control Number: 2013903743

Printed and bound in the United States of America

COVER & TEXT DESIGN by www.tothepointsolutions.com

In memory of my beautiful wife, Jody, whose passing reminded me how short life is and that unless I took the time to publish this book others would not be able to benefit from the power of these life principles.

CONTENTS

We need to be grateful for what we have today.

We need to do something nice for someone; don't wait.

We need to have an exciting goal to motivate us throughout the day.

We need to get off the fence;
make a commitment to be brave.

We need to look for the good
and take time to pray.

Preface

to Second Edition *(Written January 2015)*

I know there is a good chance I would not have had the motivation to write *The Boyne Advantage* if I hadn't done it in memory of Jody, my wife—which proves that the people who die before us can still help us.

Since the first book launch in 2013, several thousand copies have sold. Rarely does a week go by when I don't receive a note, an e-mail, a text, or someone stops me on the street, to tell me how *The Boyne Advantage* has helped them or someone they know. When people reach out like this, it affirms that the sooner we learn to stop focusing on ourselves and instead help others, we will then, and only then, begin to live life to the fullest and discover true happiness.

Following are some of the testimonials I've received. Maybe you can relate to them:

> One day as I was leaving a local restaurant, a gal stopped me to thank me for writing the book. She said she had been at odds with her brother and had not talked with him for three years. Neither of them would make the first move to make amends. She said taking the initiative was the hardest thing she had ever done. After reading *The Boyne Advantage*, she texted her brother: "I love you!" She had to wait four hours for a response. She asked me if I had any idea what his response was. I was afraid to guess. Some people hold grudges so deep and for so long they refuse to ever

make amends, even if someone else takes the first step. She said he texted back to say, "I love you too!" The gal said she doesn't know where their relationship will go, but she no longer wakes up at three in the morning wondering about him.

~

A woman I have a tremendous amount of respect for phoned me. She is an author and wrote for the local newspaper. She told me she had read *The Boyne Advantage* and it had inspired her to set new goals, again. She was so excited and wanted to thank me for writing the book. She is in her early nineties and was looking forward to new goals and all she could accomplish.

~

One of my neighbors, who was a school teacher for many years and who lives downstate most of the time, wrote me a letter to say how much she enjoyed reading the book and was grateful for its message. She wanted several copies to give to friends and family. She said she wished it had been available when she was teaching, so she could have shared it with her students.

She told me she was also dying of cancer. After reading *The Boyne Advantage*, she had set new goals of things she wanted to accomplish before she passed. And, she said it also helped her focus on one day at a time—which is all any of us really have anyway.

~

An administrator from the local school system called to ask if they could use *The Boyne Advantage* as part of the curriculum and if I would give a talk at the performing-arts center about the book. I agreed.

Afterward, I thought the talk went well considering it was only a few days before school ended and the students were focused on summer vacation. The students were polite and respectful. I was impressed with how attentive they were. Teens are not an easy audience! Each student received a copy of the book.

Later that evening, I received an e-mail from one of the parents. I was so excited. I thought she was going to tell me how inspired her son was about my talk! Instead, she said she found the book in the wastebasket and that her son was really going to get it when he got home. Meanwhile, she had read the book. She had not taken the time to set goals in a long time. She was so excited and thanked me for doing the presentation and for giving a copy to her son. (Clearly the book was meant for her.)

It's interesting how things like this happen. I know *The Boyne Advantage* isn't for everyone. A lot of it is timing. If your life is going well and you are at the top of the world, the message won't mean much. But, if you don't throw the book away, I guarantee there will be a time in your life when one of these principles will help you.

~

One day I was talking with my sister, Di. I was whining about something. I was definitely off-track. She said, "I have a suggestion. I have a book for you that might help. It's called *The Boyne Advantage*." She had me! I need to take time each day to reflect on the principles in this book to remember what I need to do to stay mentally on track.

~

I received an e-mail from a woman who owns a mortgage company. She said that she had taken many classes on motivation but the rah-rah material never seemed to work for her. She said that when she read *The Boyne Advantage*, it was different.

She was suffering the loss of her mother and her grief was so immense it consumed her. She was paralyzed with grief and it was difficult to accomplish anything positive for her or her family. Although it wasn't easy, she continued to focus on making a list of all the things she was grateful for. She scanned through the book again and knew what she needed to do. She was committed to focusing on all she had to be grateful for and, therefore, was able to contribute positively to her family that day.

Reading this book once and putting it aside won't change your life. Only by making *The Boyne Advantage* a part of your daily program will it make a positive difference in your life and thus, the lives of others.

"You can have everything in life you want if you just help enough other people get what they want."

ZIG ZIGLAR

Introduction

Several years ago, I received a gift that changed the way I look at life. It has helped me overcome tremendous challenges and allowed me to achieve dreams and goals I thought were impossible. This gift came to me as a result of an interview I had with some middle-school students in Boyne City, Michigan.

I will never forget what happened ...

At the time, I was mentally, financially, and spiritually at the lowest point I had ever been. My father, who I was very close with, had recently passed away. We had worked together, hunted together, and played guitar together. He was the leader of the band—and my best friend.

Additionally, a successful business I had owned for more than fifteen years fell on hard times. I was on the brink of losing everything. It took my life savings and all of my energy just to keep the doors open.

I felt like a failure. My self-image, self-esteem, and self-worth were at an all-time low. And I had allowed these insecurities to drive wedges in my personal relationships—even in the most important relationship I had with a beautiful lady I hoped to marry. Because of my negative attitude it wasn't long before Jody and I split and I was alone. Needless to say, I was scared, depressed, angry, frustrated, overwhelmed, and resentful.

It was about 3:30 in the afternoon on a beautiful sunny day in the middle of May. I had returned to my office after an appointment. As I was looking through my messages, one caught my eye because the number matched one of my other company phone numbers. I had been trying to get the phone company to tell me whose number it was but they refused because of confidentiality concerns. Here it was, in front of me.

Anxiously I dialed the number and asked for Nicole. When Nicole came on the line, she said she was in the eighth grade and wanted to know if I was available to meet with her. I was free for the next hour; so about twenty minutes later Nicole and a friend came to my office. They were putting together the graduation program for their class and wondered if I would be their keynote speaker. A couple of years before I had presented a goal-setting program to their class; they remembered me and thought I'd be a good candidate to speak at the eighth-grade graduation ceremony. I was honored.

We scheduled a time to meet again so we could discuss their ideas for my speech. It was during this follow-up meeting when I received the gift of which I speak and where the five basic principles—Success in Boyne—were born.

Over the years, people who were hurting; searching and reaching out for a better life; going through significant challenges; or just wanting a happier, loving, and more productive life have applied these principles and achieved success. I want to give you the same opportunity.

And, I also want to acknowledge how proud I am of Kelli. I believe she is one of the best examples of how to live by these principles.

the Boyne *Advantage*

CHAPTER 1

THE INSPIRATION

When I met with Nicole and her friend Ann, the discussion kept returning to their classmate Kelli, who was in a horrible accident the summer before. Kelli had been swimming with her brother Kyle. On her second dive off a dock, Kelli hit bottom and did not surface. Thankfully, Kyle was paying attention. He dove in and was able to get his sister out of the water before she lost consciousness.

As Kelli lay on the beach, she knew something was desperately wrong. She had no feeling from her neck down. She was rushed by ambulance to the local hospital where they made arrangements to have her airlifted to the University of Michigan Hospitals in Ann Arbor. Kelli spent the next three months there. After an operation, tests, and physical therapy, the medical professionals concluded that so much damage was done Kelli would never walk again.

Here was a twelve-year-old girl, just starting out in life, being told she would never dance at the high school prom, would not be able to walk across the stage to receive her high school diploma, and would never walk down the aisle to recite her wedding vows.

At the time I was talking with Nicole and Ann, ten months had passed since Kelli's accident. Our conversation focused on how Kelli was dealing with this life-altering event. When I asked how Kelli was doing, Nicole spoke up. "She's doing really well, Mr. Kowalske! I don't know if you knew this or not, but if it wasn't for her brother Kyle being there, she would not be here today." She then explained that the message Kelli had been conveying to her classmates was her gratitude for being alive and that she was so proud of her brother for saving her. Kelli had chosen not to focus on the fact she couldn't walk; instead she had chosen to focus on the fact that she was given a second chance.

When I heard this, I sat up in my chair as if I had been poked. You see, I was in the middle of throwing one of the biggest pity parties ever. I was whining about how unfair life was and feeling sorry for myself. As I listened to these young girls, I realized that even though I might be mentally, financially, and spiritually in a slump I had my health and I could walk.

I commented that it must be frustrating for Kelli to be so dependent on other people. Nicole looked at Ann and they both smiled. Nicole said, "We fight over who is going to carry her up and down the stairs." Evidently there were areas in the school that were not wheelchair accessible and the students would argue over who was going to help Kelli.

This made me think about my own relationships. I had just gone through a big shake-up with the company I owned and operated. About half of my staff had quit to join a competitor down the street. I was holding onto a lot of baggage from this.

"Where does she go from here?" I asked.

The girls proceeded to tell me that Kelli had two things she wanted to accomplish. The first was she wanted to graduate with her class. This was a big goal. She had spent six months in hospitals and had fallen behind. In fact, her teachers were recommending to her parents that she stay back a grade.

I said, "What's the other objective?"

"She wants to walk again," one of the girls said.

I sat up in my chair. "I thought the doctors said that was virtually impossible because of the nerve damage."

They both looked at me and said they understood, but they believed Kelli would walk again.

I remembered Earl Nightingale's definition of *success*: **the progressive realization of a worthy ideal**. Meaning if you have a goal that you are working toward at that moment, then you are successful. It doesn't matter what other craziness is going on in your life. It doesn't matter what failures you experienced in the past. If you have a goal and are focused and working on it, you are successful.

I asked Nicole and Ann if they ever wondered why these types of accidents happened to such good people. They couldn't answer this; but said that a positive result of the accident was that their class was closer and stronger, and Kelli had more appreciation and enthusiasm for life. She was driven to succeed based on her new goals; so out of this very tragic situation there was some good.

After they left, I was in awe. In forty-five minutes I had received a PhD on how life should be lived. I was impressed and inspired by Kelli's attitude, determination, commitment, and accomplishments. She was such a young person with such a big challenge. The way she handled her accident forced me to do some major soul-searching. You see, while I was whining about how unfair my life was and feeling sorry for myself, Kelli was giving thanks and being grateful for the greatest gift of all—the gift of life.

I was so excited I needed to share what I had just experienced. I walked down the hall to my assistant's office and tried to explain what had happened. I told her that God had

SUCCESS IN BOYNE

B Be grateful now.

O One person can't do it alone.

Y You choose your direction.

N Never give up.

E Every adversity holds a hidden treasure.

sent me a couple of angels with a message and an assignment. The message was a wake-up call for me to realize what was truly important in life, and the assignment was for me to organize this information so that I could easily apply and practice these principles.

It was Friday afternoon and I had to leave for another appointment; so I put the legal pad with my notes inside my briefcase. When Sunday rolled around, I woke up about 3:00 in the morning and could not get back to sleep. Sitting at the kitchen table, I opened my briefcase, took out my notes, and decided I would start organizing my speech for the graduation ceremony. In less than an hour, "Success In Boyne" was born. Although I held the pen, a power much stronger and more powerful than me did the writing.

On June 5, 1995, I addressed the eighth grade class at their evening ceremony. After the awards were handed out, I gave each student a copy of the five principles, which I called Success In Boyne (see adjacent page), and an assignment to make a list of ten things they were most grateful for and five things they had accomplished and were proud of. This list would be their personal value pack. To jump-start their day on a positive note, each morning they were to read their list. And, they should also carry a copy of their list with them so that whenever they encountered a negative situation they could refer to it and get back on track.

Because Kelli had been instrumental in inspiring me, I presented her with a framed copy of "Success in Boyne." As I handed it to Kelli, the crowd gave her a standing ovation. It was one of the most magical evenings of my life.

From these students, I received new insight, understanding, and wisdom that helped me re-prioritize and focus on the things in life that are most important. This experience gave me the push to stop wallowing in negativity and bemoaning all that was wrong with my life. I had stopped counting my blessings, stopped being grateful, stopped building relationships, stopped setting new and exciting goals, and stopped honoring commitments. I had stopped believing that regardless of the challenge Someone was watching over me.

I had stopped trusting that in the long run, with faith and a whole lot of patience, everything works out for the best.

CHAPTER 2

TESTING THE PRINCIPLES

The morning after the graduation ceremony, I started putting together my list. The first thing I did was thank God that I was alive and for giving me the opportunity to do some good. I thanked God that I could walk, see, hear, feel, and taste food—everything that I took for granted. Then I started to add things like my family, relationships, and good health. Next, I wrote down what I had done right and was proud of.

My value pack was ready. Instead of looking at what I had done wrong, I'd focus on the positive. Already I felt my self-esteem start to rise and my stress decrease. I was feeling motivated! I had jump-started my day on a positive note.

I decided to first focus on the relationships in my life—with God and with people. I had been mad at God for a long time and had stopped going to church. The simple act of being grateful for what I had finally allowed me the grace to ask God to come back into my life. I started going to church again—a move that helped improve my life in many ways.

I contacted everyone I had hurt and started to rebuild those relationships. As I mentioned, there was a lot of damage as a result of the shake-up within my company. One of the hardest things to do, is to be the first one in a damaged relationship to make an unconditional commitment to repair, strengthen, and rebuild that relationship. For the first time in a long time, I started to forgive.

Next, I took building relationships a step further and started to get involved in the community. As a result, I was awarded the Boyne Area Community Pride Civic Award by the Boyne Area Chamber of Commerce—an award given to a club, organization, or individual that has contributed much to the community that year.

I also started to set some extremely high professional goals, things I thought would be impossible to attain. As a result of this goal-setting, I was inducted into the Century 21 International Hall Of Fame, which meant I was in the top one-tenth of one percent of Century 21 real estate agents for consistent high production and quality service.

Then I began to make commitments—something that had been difficult for me to do. To begin this process, I wrote commitment letters to myself, God, and other people. As a result, on October 17, 1998, at St. Anne's Church on Mackinaw Island, at the age of forty-five, I wed Jody Anna Hill, the beautiful lady I mentioned earlier.

It was a magical day. As my wonderful bride started down the aisle on her proud father's arm, there were tears in her eyes. About three quarters of the way down, she was sobbing. By the time Jody reached the altar, she was bawling. The tears continued through most of the ceremony. As we approached the lighting of the unity candle, which is when we were to sing "From This Moment On" by Shania Twain, Jody's matron of honor was doing everything she could to keep Jody supplied with Kleenex. We got our cue and walked over to light the candle. My brother, Lon, handed each of us a microphone and we began to sing. In spite of crying, blowing her nose, and holding lots of Kleenex, Jody pulled it off beautifully.

At the end of the wedding ceremony we walked outside the church. It was an absolutely fabulous day. Awaiting us was a gorgeous, white, horse-drawn carriage. The driver wore long tails and a white top hat to match the carriage. Before we got into the carriage, there was another commitment ceremony: the release of doves. Jody and I each take a dove, recited our lines, and released the doves into the air.

We then climbed into the carriage and started our life as husband and wife.

On the days I apply these principles, there is a distinct and positive difference in the decisions and choices I make and in my actions. An example of this is one day when I was merging onto a busy interstate freeway. The driver in a car behind me was madly honking his horn and going crazy. I finally realized I must have accidentally cut him off. I had not seen him. He pulled up beside me and every window in his car went down. Even the passengers yelled at me. It was road rage at its best. My blood pressure started to rise. I really wanted to give them a piece of my mind but I knew it was my fault; so I gestured that I was sorry. It seemed like forever but he finally got the message and drove away.

I was really worked up; normally this type of altercation would have bothered me for the rest of the day. However, I started to apply the principles and within a matter of minutes I was calm and mentally back on track. I had learned that the sooner I chose to use this simple tool to cope with life's challenges, the more quickly the healing and recovery process begins and the sooner I am back in the saddle and living a constructive, positive, and meaningful life.

Although I believed in the power of these principles, I

didn't talk about them with others because I thought people would laugh—and I assumed I was the only person who needed this sort of exercise to stay positive and focused.

But, as time went on, I became aware of the stress, heartache, depression, bad relationships, lack of positive direction, and financial difficulties of the people I met. I began to wonder if, just maybe, there were others who would benefit from these principles. I decided that if I could help even one person by sharing these principles, it would be worth the time and energy invested by me to do so—even if there were some folks who thought it was silly.

So, I started to share my story; and since then, many people have attained happier lives and business success. Following are a few examples:

An old friend of mine, Bob, who lived with cerebral palsy, came to visit me at my office. His joints hurt so much he could hardly stand it. The pain medication he was taking didn't seem to help. Typically this guy was always positive. Trying to find a way to help, I decided to give Bob a copy of the five principles "Success In Boyne." I told him to take it home, read it, and call me when he could have lunch with me; then I would tell him how "Success in Boyne" came to be.

About an hour later my phone rang. He had read it over and insisted we meet soon. The following week, we met for lunch and ended up spending three hours talking about "Success In Boyne." A week later, Bob stopped by my office again. I asked him how he was doing and he said he felt great. He said, "I really don't hurt any less but I don't let it bother me as much."

In fact, Bob said he was grateful for what he did have and that he now realized that no matter how bad things were for him, there were always others who were less fortunate.

He had started to take his eyes off himself and look around at other people. He saw the blessings in his life and he was grateful for what God had given him.

A few months later, his wife called me to say that Bob had passed away during the night. She wanted to thank me for sharing the "Success In Boyne" principles with him because of how much it helped him.

I gave a copy of "Success in Boyne" to another friend, Mike, who hung it in one of the bedrooms of his vacation home in Boyne City. One of his sons had taken an executive position at Boyne USA, a well-known ski and golf resort just seven miles from their vacation home. His son told me that this was a big position and he was apprehensive about being able to perform up to his employer's expectations. He said that each morning while he ironed his clothes for the day, he would study the principles of "Success In Boyne," and then use them while on the job.

The principles helped increase his self-esteem, lowered his stress, and helped him be more positive, motivated, and focused at work. As a result, his employer was very happy with his contribution to the organization.

Another friend was a top executive in a large corporation. When I found out about his employer's financial problems and the many layoffs and plant closings, I sent him a copy of "Success In Boyne." About a week later, I talked with his wife and she said he had received it and the timing was perfect. He was so sick about what was going on at work and his potential layoff that he had gained thirty pounds. When he received the copy of "Success In Boyne" and started to apply the principles, he vowed that no matter what happened with his job, he would survive and somehow provide a good living for his family. He would not let this situation paralyze him. He would remember that he and his family were being watched over, which gave him the ability to be patient and trust everything would work out for the best. Today he has a wonderful job with another large company and doing the best ever.

FOUR YEARS LATER

The students I had addressed about the five principles were now seniors in high school and ready to graduate. Kelli invited my wife, Jody, and me to the commencement ceremony. We felt honored and looked forward to celebrating Kelli's graduation.

On the big day, when Jody and I walked into the auditorium, it was already packed. The only seats available were off to the side, with a curtain blocking our view of center stage. We felt the excitement. This class was very close. The kids were hugging and congratulating each other.

As the principal started to call the students onstage to receive their diplomas, I saw Kelli. Katie, a committed friend who had helped Kelli through thick and thin, wheeled Kelli onstage. When Kelli's name was called, the crowd went wild with applause. Then, suddenly, the crowd went quiet. You could hear a pin drop. I asked Jody if she could see what was going on. Jody said, "I don't believe this."

Behind the curtain was a walker. Katie placed it in front of Kelli and helped her stand up. At that point Kelli started the long journey across the stage. Each step took tremendous concentration. Finally, after what seemed to be an eternity, Kelli reached the podium. She stood still for a moment, reached out, and accepted her diploma! She had achieved what the doctors said could never be done. The auditorium went wild. People sprang to their feet cheering. Chills still go up and down my spine when I tell this story. Kelli had accomplished the impossible.

An interesting side note is that the class had a hard time choosing the valedictorian. It seems that 10% of the class supported a 4.0 grade point average. I would like to think that the five principles helped make that happen.

STAY FOCUSED

Let's say you are doing well, life is good, when out of the blue life throws you a challenge—a negative circumstance, disappointment, or tragedy. Boom! You get knocked off track. Instead of getting back on track, you use the obstacle as an excuse to stay unfocused. Why? Because life is tough and sometimes it seems easier to lie down in a fetal position and stay there—or hide from your problems by overeating, doing drugs, or drinking alcohol.

One of the hardest things to do is to stay focused on your goals and remain positive—especially during challenging times. What I find helpful, is that in addition to my commitment to make a conscious effort to live by these principles on a daily basis, I also share the five principles with others whenever the opportunity arises because this simple act of sharing helps me remember what I need to do to stay on track.

This might work for you, too.

the BOYNE *Advantage*

B Be grateful now. ***Don't compare yourself or your life to others.***

O One person can't do it alone. ***Surround yourself with caring, loving people.***

Y You choose your direction. ***Dream big and set goals.***

N Never give up. ***It's only failure when you stop trying.***

E Every adversity holds a hidden treasure. ***Find the silver lining.***

CHAPTER 3

THE PRINCIPLES

In a nutshell, *The Boyne Advantage* is a life- and self-improvement program that contains what I believe are the five most important success principles. When you incorporate the principles and accompanying exercises in your life, your self-esteem will increase and you will be more positive, focused, motivated, and balanced. You will feel less stressed at home and more productive at work.

These exercises stimulate and nourish your mind with what Zig Ziglar called the good, the clean, the pure, the powerful, and the positive. They give you a protective coating of strength and power to better cope with adversity, insecurity, anxiety, depression, tragedy, and ordinary day-to-day challenges.

As a result of living by these BOYNE principles (and with the help and encouragement of family, friends, and God—you see, we never do it alone, we always have help), you will accomplish things you never thought you could.

The most important gifts I received from these five principles were renewed hope, excitement, passion, appreciation, and awe for this wonderful gift of life and the realization that, in fact, there is a clock ticking and what I do between now and then is vital.

So, the question is: what will you do with the rest of your life? How do you want to live it? Will you fill your remaining days with worry; self-pity; self-doubt; resentment; conflict; and whining about how someone did you wrong, or God did you wrong to the point where there isn't enough time to do anything constructive, positive, meaningful, or helpful? Your days consist of what you choose to fill your mind with. Imagine days filled with love, comfort, appreciation, gratitude, encouragement, unconditional kindness, understanding, acceptance, forgiveness, trust and support.

You have the power to choose what you put in your mind.

One path gives you stress, heartache, depression, bad relationships, and financial difficulties. The other path brings peace, self-worth, fulfillment, enthusiasm, love, and financial abundance.

"We are who we are in life, and where we are in life is based on what has gone on in our minds. We can change who we are and change where we are heading by changing what goes into our minds."

ZIG ZIGLAR

"We become what we think about."

EARL NIGHTINGALE

PRINCIPLE 1

Be Grateful Now

Most people are grateful when something good happens, i.e., I will be grateful when I get that job. I will really be grateful when I get that raise. I will really, really be grateful when I put that big deal together. I will really, really, really be grateful when I qualify for the extreme makeover and can become a new person. I will really, really, really, really be grateful when I win the lottery.

You get the picture.

The reality, though, is life doesn't work that way.

When you are grateful for what you have *now*—no matter what is going on in your life—that is when you attract abundance.

That is how the universe works.

The upside is that it is virtually impossible to be sad or negative when you are truly grateful for all that is good.

Let me tell you a story:

There once was a farmer in South Africa. Life was good. He had a wonderful family and the farm did well enough to provide them with a comfortable life. One day, the farmer heard that people were discovering diamonds in other parts of Africa. He imagined how nice it would be if he too could mine diamonds and have all the things that money could buy.

This thought soon became an obsession. Finally, he sold the farm so he would have money to go search for diamonds and have a better life. While he was gone, he had his family live with the neighbors. Eventually his money was spent and he had not yet found any diamonds Despondent and disgusted at what he had done, he committed suicide.

Sometime later, a salesman stopped by the farm to sell seed to the new owner. The salesman noticed a stone on the mantel. As a hobby the salesman studied precious stones. He asked the farmer where he had found the huge diamond. The farmer said, "That's not a diamond. I found that stone in the backyard."

Sure enough, it was a diamond. The farm became the largest diamond mine in South Africa. The previous farmer had sold his farm for pennies to search for diamonds elsewhere. If he had only taken the time to be grateful for what he already had and looked for the many blessings around him, he would have found acres of diamonds in his own backyard.

Far too often we jump from job to job, or relationship to relationship, only to realize that if we had taken the time to look for the "diamonds" before selling out and looking elsewhere for something better, we could have saved ourselves a whole lot of wasted time and anguish.

I once heard a story about a woman who told her granddaughter that she was so blessed her cup runneth over. I like that expression. Another phrase I like is "having an attitude of gratitude." Our country has a holiday dedicated to this principle—it's called Thanksgiving!

EXERCISE FOR PRINCIPLE #1

On page 44 make a list of ten things you are grateful for and five things that you have accomplished and are proud of. Each morning before you begin your day, review this list. The simple act of reviewing your words will help you jump-start each day on a positive note.

During the day, whenever you encounter a negative or challenging situation, read the list to help you get mentally back on track.

Regularly update and add to the list. This is not a stagnate endeavor but rather an ever-changing and growing value pack.

(Note: extra worksheets are provided at the end of the book.)

B

Be grateful now.

List ten things I am grateful for and five things I am proud of accomplishing. Review this list every morning, noon, and night.

"Gratitude unlocks the fullness of life. It turns denial into acceptance, chaos to order, and confusion to clarity. It can turn a meal into a feast, a house into a home, and a stranger into a friend."

MELODY BEATTIE

PRINCIPLE 2

ONE PERSON CAN'T DO IT ALONE

Humans are spiritual beings. It is what distin-guishes us from animals. We all need a connection with a higher power. Regardless of what you believe or call your higher power, daily prayer, meditation, and/or affirmations are empowering.

I get strength from the Bible. Two of my favorite quotes are: "Everything is possible with God." (Mark 10:27) and "I can do all things through Christ who strengthens me." (Philippians 4:13) When I connected with God, I was luckier and everything in my life started to fall into place. Find your spiritual connection.

One simple but great affirmation is to simply say thank you. The motivating power of these two words is amazing.

The second part of this principle is your relationship with other people. You need to start building and rebuilding your relationships. People tend to carry around old baggage and harbor hard feelings and resentments that they are too proud or stubborn to let go of. Everyone does it in one degree or another. However, this negativity is like poison and it makes you sick so you can't perform good works throughout the day. One of the most difficult things to do is to be the first one in a damaged relationship to say I'm sorry and to make an unconditional commitment to repair, strengthen, and rebuild that relationship.

Don't let your ego get in the way of allowing happiness in your life.

I have a friend whose husband divorced her years ago. To this day she cannot forgive him. She continues to degrade him in front of their children, which puts a lot of stress on their visits with her and family gatherings. The children dread seeing their mother. Meanwhile, she is miserable most of the time because she continues to tote around all of this baggage.

You need to do the opposite. Forgiveness is a powerful motivating tool. You cannot truly love until you rid yourself of these feelings. You will benefit once you set yourself free of the negativity.

A great exercise I learned came from a retired chaplain who headed up a prison ministry. It is simple. On a piece of paper, make a list of the people you are at odds with or hold some type of resentment against. You can also include something that you haven't forgiven yourself for. When you are finished writing, take the list outside and burn it. Then, every time you begin to think about the resentment or hard feelings toward those people or yourself, remember that you burned the resentment and it no longer exists.

A good example about making a difference are these two stories:

A young boy was walking along the beach. The tide had receded and there were hundreds of starfish that were stranded and soon to die. One by one, the boy was throw-

ing them back into the cool water so they could survive. An older man who was also was walking along the beach saw what the young boy was doing. He said, "Why are you doing that? You can't possibly make a difference. Look, there are hundreds."

The boy slowly looked up at the man, picked up another starfish, threw it back into the water, and said, "It makes a difference to this one."

~ ~

My brother helps people with substance abuse. He says it is heart-breaking that the percentage of those who stay in recovery for a long period of time is so low. But he doesn't give up on them. He advises everyone in recovery to focus on one day at a time—until they have many years of sobriety under their belt and have accomplished wonderful things for themselves and helped other people because of their recovery.

One day at a time is a great way for all of us to live. That's all we have anyway. Just today!

You need to live the best you can today and not worry about tomorrow until tomorrow.

I shall pass through this world but once,
Any good therefore that I can do,
Any kindness that I can show to any human being let me do it now,
let me not defer it,
nor neglect it,
for I shall not pass this way again.

STEPHEN GRELLET

EXERCISE FOR PRINCIPLE #2

The exercise is simple but not easy to do: apologize, forgive, or do something nice for at least one person every day.

Start by making a list of the people you need to forgive or apologize to, including yourself if necessary, on the adjacent page (or a separate piece of paper). Then burn the list—with the understanding that you have forgiven everyone on the list and will begin to rebuild those relationships. Realize that even with all of your efforts to rebuild a relationship, sometimes a person will not accept your apology—but you need to continue to make the effort for you.

Example:

> *Years ago, a dear friend and employee quit my company over some misunderstandings and office politics. I received a hate letter like you couldn't believe. Determined to rebuild the relationship, I went to her house. I knocked on the door and when she opened it and saw it was me she slammed the door in my face. I don't know what possessed me, but I knocked on the door and yelled, "You can hate me all you want, but I will love you till the day I die." When she opened the door, she was crying. She didn't know what to say, so she asked me what I wanted in my coffee. To this day, we continue to be best of friends.*

(Note: extra worksheets are provided at the end of the book.)

O

One person can't do it alone.

We need to forgive and give service. Who can I help today? Who do I need to apologize to? Do it now!

PRINCIPLE 3

YOU CHOOSE YOUR DIRECTION

The power to choose is the greatest gift God gave humans—it is called "free will." The first time I heard of this principle was when I read a book by Earl Nightingale called *Your Greatest Power*. Nightingale wrote about the gift that God gave us; Nightingale called it the "Power of Choice." We have the freedom to make choices that will benefit us or choices that will hurt us and set us back.

Understanding the power of free will and choice helped me immensely—even in my real estate career. Taking ownership of your personal and business decisions is empowering.

An example of someone who lived by this principle was my mother. When she was fifty-three years old, she started to feel pain in her back. It would not go away. After having it checked out by a doctor, she received the worst news you could imagine: there was a tumor the size of a football on her spine and it was cancerous. In ninety days, Mom took a turn for the worst. In the hospital and under an oxygen tent, she was in tremendous pain. The doctors gave her only a few days to live. Mom told my sisters, Diane and Martha, to call some of her friends to come visit her before she passed on.

One of Mom's friends was Father Denny. When he got there, he looked at Mom in the oxygen tent and said, "Elaine, you are always smiling!"

Without hesitation, Mom said, "I do so, because I choose so."

Talk about understanding the power of choice.

Once you accept the fact that people have free will—the ability to choose—you need to establish life and business goals and a specific plan to take you in the direction of your goals. (In fact, Thomas Edison, Henry Ford, and John D. Rockefeller always had written goals that they reviewed daily.)

Zig Ziglar believed that to be well-rounded, people need to set goals in six areas. These areas are:

SPIRITUAL

FAMILY

MENTAL

PHYSICAL

FINANCIAL

SOCIAL

Ziglar also said the following nine components are required to achieve maximum results while working toward your goals.

1. **Each goal must be in writing.** Take the time to ponder what you want in life, put it in writing, and focus on it until it becomes reality. Our minds work in specifics and we can easily forget things; thus, the first step is to write down your goals.

2. **Goals must be specific.** For example, rather than having the goal to be "number one in sales" it is more helpful to establish a specific number, i.e., "I will achieve $20,000 in weekly sales." Also, you need to devise a plan on how you are going to achieve each goal. If you are a student and have a goal to earn a grade point average of 3.5 for the semester, write down how this can be accomplished.

3. **Goals must be demanding enough to excite you.**

4. **Goals must be achievable.** For example, for me to want to become an Olympic downhill skier is foolhardy. I am too old to compete against the younger and physically fit athletes. I could, however, set a goal of doing other races.

5. **Goals must be measurable.** Each goal must be broken down into daily or weekly tasks that lead to completion.

6. **Goals must be visible.** Your list of goals must be where you can see it every day, i.e., taped to the bathroom mirror, on your cell phone, or on your computer screen. Out of sight, out of mind is not beneficial for reaching your goals.

7. **Goals must have a time frame.** A goal without a completion date could take forever to accomplish. Establish deadlines for each goal. Publishing this book has been a goal for several years. Until I set a deadline to finish it, I knew it would probably never happen.

8. **Goals must be shared with people you trust.** Let the people who support you know your goals. It can be family members, friends, coworkers, a personal development coach, or members of a business or support group. Sharing your goals with people you trust will help you stay accountable.

9. **A completed goal must be celebrated.** Reward yourself when you achieve your goals. Follow the if-then formula: If I accomplish _______, then I will do/get this as a reward. Knowing there is a reward waiting will keep you motivated as you work toward your goals. Imagine yourself celebrating the achievement.

There once was a wise old man who lived near a lake. One day, a young man came to the sage and said, "Someone told me that you could tell me the secret to success in life." The sage took the young man down to the lake and asked the young man to put his head under the water. When he did so, the sage put his hands on the young man's submerged head and held it there until the young man summoned every ounce of strength to break free from his grasp and pull his head from the water. As the young man sat down, gasping for breath, the sage said, "If you want success as much as you wanted that breath of air, you will have found the secret!"

EXERCISE FOR PRINCIPLE #3

Write down at least one goal in the six areas of your life (see list on page 54) and follow the nine steps for each.

(Note: extra worksheets are provided at the end of the book.)

Y

You choose your direction.
(For a well-balanced life.)

Set a goal in at least one area of your life—spiritual, family, mental, physical, financial, or social. Be sure to apply the nine components on pages 55-56.

Goals & Activities Flow Chart

Practice the *if-then* principle: *If* I work on or accomplish _______, *then* I will reward myself by __________.

9 Components to Achieving Goals:

1. In writing
2. Specific
3. Demanding
4. Achievable
5. Measurable
6. Visible
7. Time Frame
8. Shared
9. Celebrated

Step 1: My goal is: ____________________

Step 2: Obstacles (negative people, etc.) are: _____

Step 3: Deadline for completion: __________

Step 4: What I must do each day/week: _______

Step 5: Time I will set aside each day/week:

Step 6: My rewards (free time, etc.) each day/week:

Step 7: My reward on achieving this goal: _______

Step 8: I will display this goal flow chart: _______

Step 9: Trusted supporters to share this goal with:

Goals help you accomplish more. The more you accomplish, the better you like yourself. The better you like yourself, the better you like others. – ZIG ZIGLAR

Goals & Activities Flow Chart

Practice the *if-then* principle: *If* I work on or accomplish _______, *then* I will reward myself by _________.

9 Components to Achieving Goals:

1. In writing
2. Specific
3. Demanding
4. Achievable
5. Measurable
6. Visible
7. Time Frame
8. Shared
9. Celebrated

Step 1: My goal is: _______________

Step 2: Obstacles (negative people, etc.) are: _______________

Step 3: Deadline for completion: _______________

Step 4: What I must do each day/week: _______________

Step 5: Time I will set aside each day/week: _______________

Step 6: My rewards (free time, etc.) each day/week: _______________

Step 7: My reward on achieving this goal: _______________

Step 8: I will display this goal flow chart: _______________

Step 9: Trusted supporters to share this goal with: _______________

Goals help you accomplish more. The more you accomplish, the better you like yourself. The better you like yourself, the better you like others. - ZIG ZIGLAR

Goals & Activities Flow Chart

Practice the *if-then* principle: *If* I work on or accomplish _______, *then* I will reward myself by _________.

9 Components to Achieving Goals:

1. In writing
2. Specific
3. Demanding
4. Achievable
5. Measurable
6. Visible
7. Time Frame
8. Shared
9. Celebrated

Step 1: My goal is: ____________________

Step 2: Obstacles (negative people, etc.) are: ____

Step 3: Deadline for completion: ____________

Step 4: What I must do each day/week: ________

Step 5: Time I will set aside each day/week:

Step 6: My rewards (free time, etc.) each day/week:

Step 7: My reward on achieving this goal: ________

Step 8: I will display this goal flow chart: ________

Step 9: Trusted supporters to share this goal with:

Goals help you accomplish more. The more you accomplish, the better you like yourself. The better you like yourself, the better you like others. – ZIG ZIGLAR

PRINCIPLE 4

Never Give Up

Winston Churchill gave the following commencement speech at a university:

"Never, never, never, never give up."

That was the whole speech, in its entirety.

I have heard this same advice from motivational coaches and other successful people. It is the commitment you make that will give you the enthusiasm and the energy to stay the course.

No matter what happens, never give up on yourself.

When things go wrong, as they sometimes will,
When the road you're trudging seems all uphill,
When the funds are low and the debts are high,
And you want to smile, but you have to sigh,
When care is pressing you down a bit,
Rest, if you must, but don't you quit.

**Life is queer with its twists and turns,
As every one of us sometimes learns,
And many a failure turns about,
When he might have won had he stuck it out;
Don't give up though the pace seems slow—
You may succeed with another blow.**

**Often the goal is nearer than,
It seems to a faint and faltering man,
Often the struggler has given up,
When he might have captured the victor's cup,
And he learned too late when the night
slipped down,
How close he was to the golden crown.**

**Success is failure turned inside out—
The silver tint of the clouds of doubt,
And you never can tell how close you are,
It may be near when it seems so far,
So stick to the fight when you're hardest hit—
It's when things seem worst that you must
not quit.**

AUTHOR UNKNOWN

EXERCISE FOR PRINCIPLE #4

Get off the fence and make a commitment to be brave! Write a letter to yourself, to God, or someone else promising to pursue your goals—and sign it.

(Note: extra worksheets are provided at the end of the book.)

N

Never give up.

Write a commitment letter to myself, my spouse, a friend, a coworker, or a higher power—and sign it.

PRINCIPLE 5

Every Adversity Holds a Hidden Treasure

Truthfully, this principle is the one I struggle with the most—but I do believe wholeheartedly that with faith and patience, all of us can recover. Regardless of your situation, you must trust that eventually life will work itself out; that something positive will come from the adversity. I am not suggesting that all life experiences are easy and I am not minimizing your pain, loss, or struggle.

Oftentimes after being dealt an especially difficult challenge, you need to allow time to pass before you can actually see the positive that God has in store. I know that the sooner you choose to search for the positive, the easier it will be to cope; the quicker the healing and recovery process begins; and the sooner you will get back on track so you can start doing something constructive, positive, and meaningful.

Jody once shared with me that God only gives three answers to our prayers: yes, not yet, or I have something better planned for you. Believe in God's plan. Do your best; give God the rest.

EXERCISE FOR PRINCIPLE #5

Focus on three adversities that you experienced and find three positive outcomes from each. Then write down the adversities you are now living through and imagine the positive outcomes.

(Note: extra worksheets are provided at the end of the book.)

E

Every adversity holds a hidden treasure.

Things happen for a reason. List one adverse experience and three positive things that happened as a result (look for the silver lining).

In a Nutshell:

Be grateful for what you have today.

Do something nice for someone. Don't wait!

Have an exciting goal to give you energy and motivate you throughout the day.

Get off the fence. Make a commitment; be brave.

Look for the good in life and people; take time to meditate or pray.

Conclusion

After seventeen brief years together, my wife, passed away. Jody was only forty-three. She was the greatest thing that ever happened to me. I really did not start living life until I met Jody. She opened my eyes to what life had to offer. Jody was the love of my life.

Losing Jody caused me the most pain and sadness I had ever experienced. There were days when I wondered how I could go on living; if I could survive. Then, one day at her grave site, when I was trying to calm my aching heart, I looked around and noticed the graves of children who had died. I could only imagine the pain parents experience when losing a child.

Like a bolt of lightning, I remembered the lessons that I had learned years ago with my discussions with Nicole and Ann about Kelli: No matter what the situation is and how bad things are, you can always find other people who are hurting worse than you. Regardless of the pain and loss, you have the power to choose how you look at and handle any situation. No matter the situation, you can always find something to be grateful for. Not only is it possible—it is imperative to the healing and recovery process.

As I stood by Jody's grave, I realized I was one of the luckiest guys on earth. And, once I thanked God for the blessing of Jody in my life, my healing began. It was the hardest thing I ever had to go through, but I was finally on the road to becoming more productive and being able to help others. I made the decision to finally put this story to print so that it could be shared with you.

In closing, I'd like to share some wise words I once heard Zig Ziglar recite. They are a good summary of the message in this book:

God said to build a better world
and I said, "How?"

It's such a tough time to make a living
and life itself is so complicated now.

With family, work, social, and worldwide
issues there is so much to do.

But God, in all His wisdom, said,
"Just build a better YOU!"

Extra Worksheets

For your convenience, I am providing the five principles combined on one page and extra worksheets that can be copied and scanned.

the BOYNE *Advantage*

B — Be grateful now. ***Don't compare yourself or your life to others.***

O — One person can't do it alone. ***Surround yourself with caring, loving people.***

Y — You choose your direction. ***Dream big and set goals.***

N — Never give up. ***It's only failure when you stop trying.***

E — Every adversity holds a hidden treasure. ***Find the silver lining.***

The BOYNE Advantage

5 Simple Steps for Achieving Success in Work and Life

B	O	Y	N	E
Be grateful now.	One person can't do it alone.	You choose your direction.	Never give up.	Every adversity holds a hidden treasure.
List things I am grateful for and things I am proud of accomplishing.	**Build strong relationships. List people I can help or apologize to.**	**Set spiritual, family, mental, physical, financial, and social goals.**	**Write at least three commitment letters.**	**List adverse experiences and three positive things that resulted.**

Signature ____________ Date ____________

Signature of trusted friend or mentor ____________ Date ____________

Nine Components to Achieving Your Goals:

In writing • Specific • Demanding • Achievable • Measurable • Visible • Time Frame • Shared • Celebrated

The BOYNE Advantage

5 Simple Steps for Achieving Success in Work and Life

B	O	Y	N	E
Be grateful now.	One person can't do it alone.	You choose your direction.	Never give up.	Every adversity holds a hidden treasure.
List things I am grateful for and things I am proud of accomplishing.	**Build strong relationships. List people I can help or apologize to.**	**Set spiritual, family, mental, physical, financial, and social goals.**	**Write at least three commitment letters.**	**List adverse experiences and three positive things that resulted.**

Signature ______ Date ______

Signature of trusted friend or mentor ______ Date ______

Nine Components to Achieving Your Goals:

In writing • Specific • Demanding • Achievable • Measurable • Visible • Time Frame • Shared • Celebrated

B

Be grateful now.

List ten things I am grateful for and five things I am proud of accomplishing. Review this list every morning, noon, and night.

O

One person can't do it alone.

We need to forgive and give service. Who can I help today? Who do I need to apologize to? Do it now!

Y

You choose your direction.
(For a well-balanced life.)

Set a goal in at least one area of your life—spiritual, family, mental, physical, financial, or social. Be sure to apply the nine components on pages 55-56.

N

Never give up.

Write a commitment letter to myself, my spouse, a friend, a coworker, or a higher power—and sign it.

E

Every adversity holds a hidden treasure.

Things happen for a reason. List one adverse experience and three positive things that happened as a result (look for the silver lining).

Goals & Activities Flow Chart

Practice the *if-then* principle: *If* I work on or accomplish _______, *then* I will reward myself by __________.

9 Components to Achieving Goals:

1. In writing
2. Specific
3. Demanding
4. Achievable
5. Measurable
6. Visible
7. Time Frame
8. Shared
9. Celebrated

Step 1: My goal is: ______________________

Step 2: Obstacles (negative people, etc.) are: ____

Step 3: Deadline for completion: ___________

Step 4: What I must do each day/week: _________

Step 5: Time I will set aside each day/week:

Step 6: My rewards (free time, etc.) each day/week:

Step 7: My reward on achieving this goal: _______

Step 8: I will display this goal flow chart: _______

Step 9: Trusted supporters to share this goal with:

Goals help you accomplish more. The more you accomplish, the better you like yourself. The better you like yourself, the better you like others. – ZIG ZIGLAR

Goals & Activities Flow Chart

Practice the *if-then* principle: *If* I work on or accomplish _______, *then* I will reward myself by _________.

9 Components to Achieving Goals:

1. In writing
2. Specific
3. Demanding
4. Achievable
5. Measurable
6. Visible
7. Time Frame
8. Shared
9. Celebrated

Step 1: My goal is: ____________________

Step 2: Obstacles (negative people, etc.) are: ____

Step 3: Deadline for completion: ____________

Step 4: What I must do each day/week: ________

Step 5: Time I will set aside each day/week:

Step 6: My rewards (free time, etc.) each day/week:

Step 7: My reward on achieving this goal: _______

Step 8: I will display this goal flow chart: _______

Step 9: Trusted supporters to share this goal with:

Goals help you accomplish more. The more you accomplish, the better you like yourself. The better you like yourself, the better you like others. – ZIG ZIGLAR

ACKNOWLEDGMENT

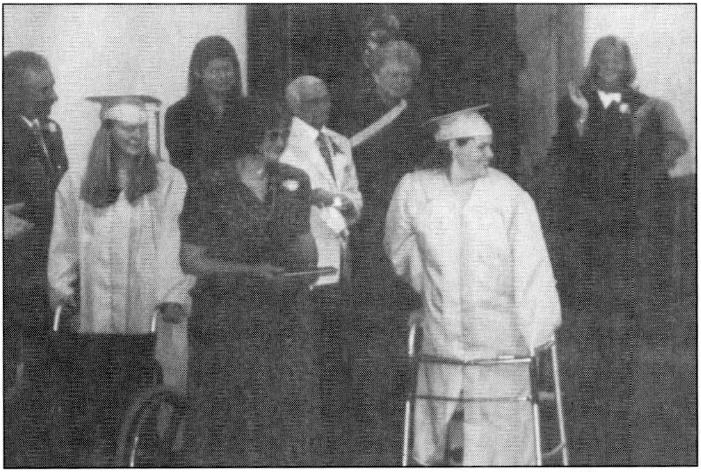

Kelli walks across the stage to receive her high school diploma—six years after doctors told her she'd never walk again. (June 4, 1999)

Kelli paid a high personal price at a young age and nothing I or anyone else says can change that. What I can and do say is thank you, Kelli, for your inspiration. Your life is the epitome of what can happen when someone lives by the principles of *The Boyne Advantage.*

You made an impact on my life—and I know when others live by the principles in this book, they too will experience positive change.

About the Author

Mark D. Kowalske lives and is involved in the community of Boyne City, Michigan. With twenty years on the planning board, he helped form the Downtown Development Authority and the Main Street Program. Mark was also the creator and sponsor of the Boyne City Slogan Contest which produced over 720 entries with the winning slogan: Home Town Feel, Small Town Appeal. Mark was also creator of the Boyne City Song Contest where 72 songs were written about Boyne City.

Mark's community involvement helped him receive the prestigious Boyne Area Community Civic Pride Award.

Mark earned a GRI designation and was inducted into the Who's Who in Real Estate in America at the young age of thirty. Later he founded and brokered a Century 21 office for nearly twenty years and was inducted into the Century 21 International Hall of Fame.

Most recently Mark has taken a position as Associate Broker with Coldwell Banker Schmidt Realtors.

In his spare time, he enjoys playing music with his sister, Diane, and his brother, Lon, in the Kowalske Family Band.

Availability to Speak

Mark Kowalske believes in the value and power of these five principles and is available to present them to individuals or groups as part of a seminar or other event.

If you or your organization are interested in having Mark present *The Boyne Advantage*, please contact him via phone (231-675-3721) or email (markkowalske@gmail.com).